THE BOWERY

THE BOWERY

Michael D. Zettler

DRAKE PUBLISHERS INC.
NEW YORK · LONDON

Published in 1975 by
Drake Publishers, Inc.
381 Park Avenue South
New York, New York, 10016

Copyright (c) 1975 by Mike Zettler.
All rights reserved.

Library of Congress Cataloging in Publication Data

Zettler, Mike.
  The Bowery.

  1. Alcoholics — New York (City). 2. New York (City) — Streets — Bowery. 3. New York (City) — Social conditions. I. Title.
HV5298.N5Z48   309.1'747'1   74-22604
ISBN 0-87749-735-4

Printed in the United States of America.

1 2 3 4 5 6 7 8 9 0

There are several people who helped immeasurably in the preparation of this book. These are but a few:

> MICHAEL SIMONE, who started me on the path I have chosen by many years ago taking the time to tell me what my eyes and ears were to be used for.
>
> ALLAN GREEN and OLAF OHANSON, who always come up with the right answers to my photographic problems.
>
> KINGDON LANE at Spiratone.
>
> JULIE and MILTON at JayDee Camera.
>
> THE GREAT YELLOW GOD from Rochester and their excellent technical staffs.
>
> LEONARD JACKSON at the New York City Bureau of Correction.
>
> DR. DOMINICK De MAIO and his staff at the New York City Medical Examiners Office.
>
> MY WIFE who has always thought my pictures were . . .
>   "Really nice."

This book is dedicated to L.G.

INTRODUCTION

Literally, the Bowery, on New York's lower east side, is a two-way street that runs north-south starting at Astor Place. Through the years it has taken on other meanings and now the name brings thoughts of winos, down-and-outers, . . . The end of the line. Those images are not without validity, and if you should go there, or just wake up there, you won't be disappointed. Whatever you're looking for in the way of pain, torment, and degradation is on open display, available to the general public, if you will. What the rest of us would try so desperately to hide, is here out in the open. And that's what makes the Bowery unique. There is little pretence here; these men are alchoholics, drunks, and most readily acknowledge this, referring to themselves in the most self-disparaging terms possible. Unable to cope with a world that seems to have little time for them or their problems, they retreat to the safety of wine and kindred souls, . . . The Bowery.

Once on the Bowery living is cheap. In the summer sleep outside; if you have to take the time to eat there are shelters and missions that don't ask much in return for feeding. Companionship? Plenty. If you need medical help wait til it gets really bad or until you break something else, someone will pick you up and take you to one of the city hospitals. Wine; 77 cents a pint. In the Winter it gets a bit more expensive, but life gets cheaper. It's tough on the Bowery. It hurts. A very high tolerance for pain is essential, it's everywhere, always within easy reach. The demons that ride herd on the men sober are little more painful than the sensation of alchohol poured into ulcerated bellys and malfunctioning kidneys and livers. There are more crutches per square foot on the Bowery than any place outside of medical facilities in the city. Open dirt-encrusted wounds, filthy dressings, or no dressing at all are the norm. . . . What makes all this even more painful is that every man knows the way out of the Bowery. Most try putting down the bottle from time to time, but almost all return before calling it quits.

Freedom may seem a funny word to use in connection with these men, but there certainly is a perverse sense of freedom that pervades this street. Once you've reached bottom what the hell can you say or do to make it worse? The only concerns are a couple of pints for tomorrow, and there's no point in thinking about it until tomorrow comes. This freedom allows any topic open for conversation with none of the face-saving preliminaries found at country clubs and barbeques or any of the other places drinkers assemble. Here you say what you've got to say and be done with it.

There are many sincere, selfless, hardworking people involved in a score of private and public agencies to try and bring some form of relief to the Bowery. Unfortunately, they can do little but bind up the wounds and tend to whatever physical needs the men will allow them to. The real pain is deep inside, inaccessible to hot meals, clean clothes or a place out of the cold. The problem is made even more difficult by the intelligence of the men. These are not dumb people; the average intelligence is way above that of any random sample. Most are reasonably well educated, and what can be found of the brain after the alchohol has done its work is perceptive and eager to voice an opinion on an amazingly wide variety of subjects . . . They know that the bottle is only part of the problem. The demons are the other part and heaven knows where they come from . . . so until they find a way to get rid of the demons all together, the bottle will have to stay, to at least keep them from the door.

There are problems in doing a study of the Bowery. The primary one was handling my own emotions. The first full day spent there accosts the senses like a man with a sledge hammer. Here are the obvious sights, those you half expect, but there is nothing that quite prepares you to sit down in the gutter with a man who has vomited his last three meals onto his overcoat, possibly pissed himself several times, and talk about the state of the world. The natural instinct is to take him and wash and clothe and feed this man, . . . Help him somehow. After a while you learn that he can get all that in a dozen other places, what he wants from you is someone to talk to, relive old glories and defeats; . . . Someone who isn't being paid to do it. Someone who will sit and treat him like another human being.

There were other problems. Whenever you inject an alien presence into a community such as this, tight situations occur. In the end the one thing that always seemed to get me out was the truth. Why me telling a man that I sincerely cared what happened to him would make him put a knife away I don't know . . . Other than it was the truth. But the minor scuffles and incidents are interesting little stories to joke about, a tap dance to get you out. They don't come back to you in the middle of the night. Late one snowy night I was heading home, back uptown, when I came past a bar I knew. In front a man had collapsed and passed out on his crutches. With the snow piling up around him I rolled him over and stupidly asked whether he was all right. He said he was. I asked him where he was going to spend the night . . .

"Right here."

"You can't."

"Yeah? . . . You gonna go a buck and a quarter for a room??"

I had a subway token. Once again I was confronted with the reality that not everybody sleeps warmly under a nice middle-class electric blanket. Five men froze that night. When I first arrived on the Bowery and told an old hand what I was about, he told me, "The time will come for you to leave and I doubt you'll be back."

"When will that be?"

"You'll know . . . There's something that tells you 'It's time to go'."

I went from the horror and repulsion at human beings in this kind of agony to feeling and caring enough to try and do something, to acceptance of this way of life as an alternative, and then one day not that long ago I was standing one block north of Delancy and a man at least five years my junior came toward me. He had open sores on his face, parts of his skin were going black. One of his eyes was completely red. I looked and was about to reach for one of my cameras when I stopped . . . Was there something unique? Photographically striking? . . . My advance money was long gone and now nearing the end I was running out of supplies. I didn't take the picture. His agony was too close to the norm. It wouldn't prove a point any better than what I already had.

That was the last day I spent on the Bowery.

> You know there's lots a very beautiful buildings down here . . . What they ought to do is put us bums to work clearing the mess up. Then it would be beautiful like it used to be . . . I seen pictures once in the bank; Beautiful ladies and carriages . . . You think I'm kidding you . . . It's the truth. I swear it . . . All this was once beautiful.

"I'm here by choice . . . That's right . . . Gotta make the choice, the wine or the job . . . I used to have a good car, lots of clothes . . . Yeah me! . . . One time my girls says to me, "Artie, it's either me or the wine!" . . . I says, "I hate to tell you this sweetie . . . But so long."

> There's always hope ain't there . . . I mean we're all goin' to get out a here ain't we . . . I mean . . . Sometime. Right?

In the winter time it's a bitch . . . They all got the windows up . . .
'course now all the cars is air conditioned so it's tough in the
summer too.

"I might be a dishwasher up in the mountains but I'll tell you something . . . . In New York I go strictly first class . . . "

THE BOWERY 11

"Not '58!! The last time I fought in the garden was '48. 1947!! I fought on some damn good cards then . . . I was never a boxer though . . . A fighter. I'm still a fighter. It's all I know how to do. If I ever lost it was because I didn't hit 'em, 'cause when I hit 'em they stayed hit."

"Times is rough Son, real tough . . . What's a dollar buy you today? . . . Not much and I'll tell you that . . . I remember a quarter'd buy you a string of fish, almost touch the ground."

"Where's that?"

"Charleston . . . Good fish, too."

THE BOWERY 17

I'd much rather be outside but the sun hurts my eyes . . . that's the truth too, doctor told me to keep out of the sun.

"My best friend in the whole world is an N.Y.U. professor. He's the smartest man in the world. I used to wait for him every morning and we'd have long talks on his way to class . . . I'd be there every morning no matter what. One time it was snowing and I lost my shoes but I went anyway . . . He gave me a five dollar bill once and I never went to see him again . . . He was so fucking smart he didn't know I was his friend."

"Yeah, it's my dog . . . You can call him Blackie . . . or Whitie . . . He's my dog."

"He bite?"

"Naw. He won't bite long as I say so."

"He's yours?"

"He ain't really my dog . . . He ain't nobody's."

"Sometimes I guess it's good company."

"It ain't that. It's good 'cause nobody messes with you . . . He'll protect you from people trying to steal your shoes . . . Got to like dogs though . . . Cocker spaniels are good . . . They got good hair for sleeping in the cold."

"What happens when you go outside?"

"He knows where you are . . . Hell, he can smell your piss and vomit three blocks away . . . I guess you can smell it too, hunh? . . . Difference is you think we all smell alike, he knows it's me."

"What do you feed him?"

"I don't feed him nothing."

"Nothing?"

"Hell, I don't feed myself nothing."

You must learn the art. The art of staying alive and staying drunk . . . Alcohol is essential my friend. It is a tool to be used in the greatest art of them all; loosing certain memories, getting rid of the excess baggage if you will . . . But here comes the catch—if you loose all the memories you won't have a reason to drink. . . . That is a problem, isn't it?

"You see them guys on the news talking about the people wasting the land and all that ecology stuff. They ought to come down here and talk to some of us about that. We don't waste nothing. You can't afford to waste nothing. It takes too much to get it together enough to get something done to waste none of it. It might seem strange to you, but drunks is real careful. You watch one coming out of a store sometime. You never see him carry no bottle. He might drop it. He puts it as deep in his clothing as possible, that way it's cushioned when he falls . . . Never leave the cap off the bottle neither, that way when you knock it over it won't spill . . . Best is to put the cap on real tight and lay the bottle down, or put it back in your pocket. Got to be careful with your body too, especially the legs. If you get on crutches there ain't nobody going to serve you, not the bars and not the stores. Drunks know how to conserve things."

THE BOWERY 27

"Really, I need it for food. I ain't shitting you. I'm going over to mission street to see if my welfare check come . . . It ain't never going to come . . . Man, If I could only get it together a little bit I'd get out of this town . . . Hell, I'd get out of this country. London, maybe France or California . . . My mom lives there . . . Stockton . . . I should go back there . . . I lived there three years . . . Man, if I could only steal a Cadillac. I'd be fat man, fat . . . I'd go to California sure then. . . . . . . For sure."

THE BOWERY   29

"Hey Pal!! . . . I hate to bother you, I normally don't do this but . . . I'm a little short and I wondered if you could help me out with four cents . . . All I need is four more cents . . . I wouldn't lie to you friend . . . It ain't for food. I got seventy-three cents and I need four more. . . . You'ld really be helping me out Pal."

THE BOWERY 31

"I'm sure he's coming. I'm telling you, you can set your watch by him. 12:15 every weekday . . . Yup! There he is. In the grey suit. With the two broads . . . What is it?"

"12:19"

"Four minutes off. That ain't bad. He'll take them two over to the hotel and stay in there until exactly 1:55 . . . You can set your watch by that too. . . . See the bag? You might think he's got booze. No Sir. He gets that from the deli. Same every day; pastrami on rye and a diet soda. I asked the guy behind the counter."

"Always the same women?"

"Naw. He switches 'em around. Last spring he was going in there with nothing but chinee, but I ain't seen him with a chink in a long time."

"Every day?"

"I tell you you can set your watch. He's got a lighting fixture store down by Broome. He gets out at twelve and goes down to Canal and gets two hooks, over to the deli, then at 12:15 he hits the hotel 'til 1:55. Been doing it for years. I tell ya, you can set your watch by it."

THE BOWERY 33

I eat when I have to . . . I hate to spend money for it, especially when you're having trouble keeping it down.

"Hello Kathleen?? . . . It's Frankie . . . I swear to God I ain't touched nothing in over a month . . . I swear to God . . . I don't want nothing. . . I just wanted to talk, that's all . . . How's Mom? . . . No it ain't my fault . . . I can't go see her . . . I just can't!!! . . . Don't hang up on me!!! . . . Please . . . I ain't got another dime to call you back . . . Please! . . . KATHLEEN?!?!?! . . . She don't care neither . . . My own flesh and blood and she don't care."

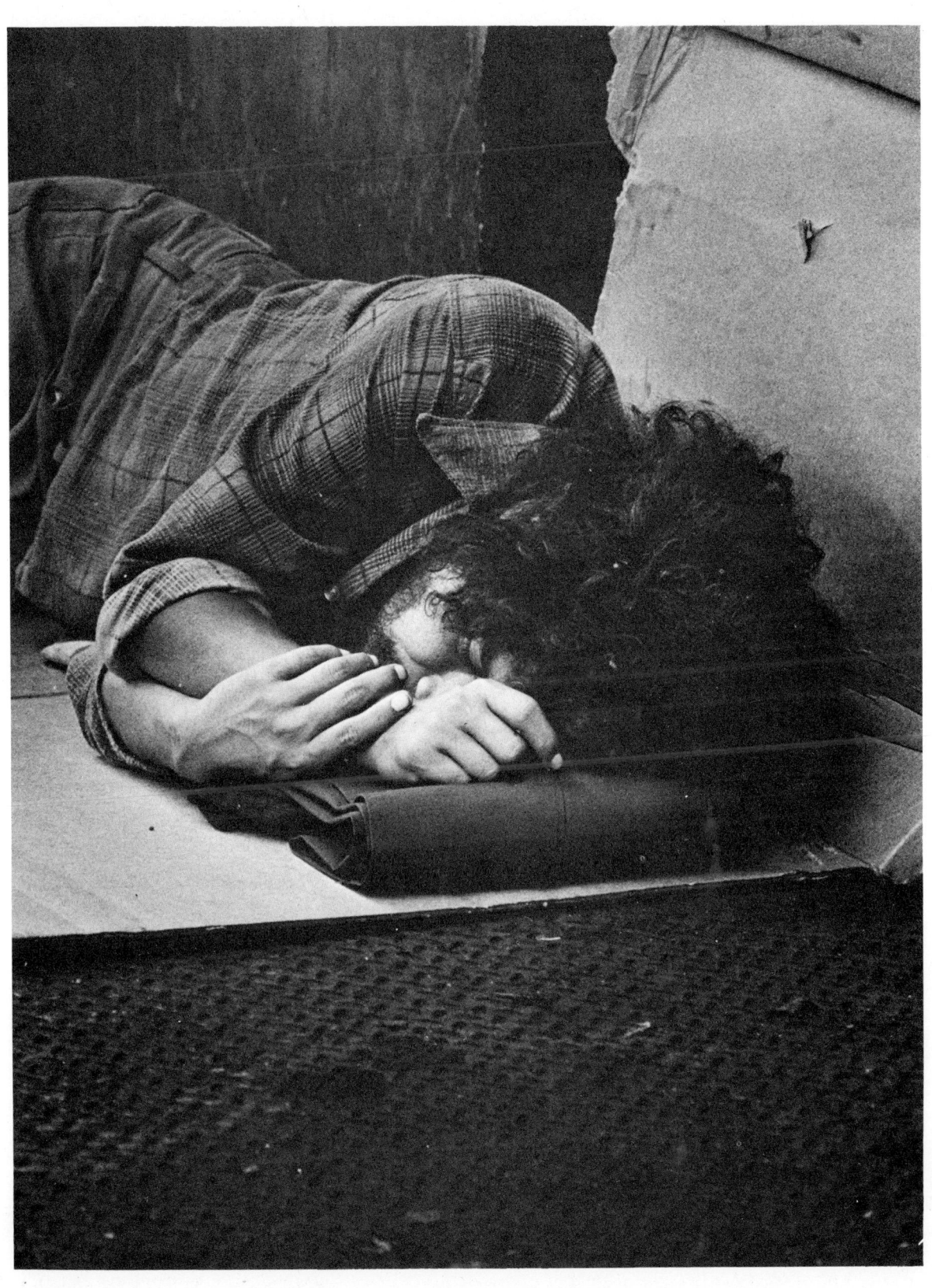

"They sent me over to see them at the clinic on front street. The elevator was broken. Then never work in them old buildings. It took me nearly an hour to get up to the fourth floor. I went up to this nurse sitting there, at least she looked like a nurse . . . The white hat and everything. Well, she let me tell her the whole problem then she tells me I got to go back to the welfare and get this form. I told her the elevator was broke but she says it ain't her problem. I told her to fuck herself, but I don't think she heard me. And when I go back the next day they still ain't got the elevator fixed. This time when I get up there this fuckin' . . . I guess I shouldn't say that. She tells me they aren't supposed to take care of me. I got to go all the way up to city hospital . . . Now why do you suppose she did that?"

"Naw. The kids don't fuck with the bowery bums . . . and it ain't just because we ain't got nothing . . . They respect us. They know we seen it all . . . Their parents tell 'em not to fuck with the bums too. They respect us. That's the truth too . . . . . . What good is it anyway, we ain't got nothing, we ain't nobody . . . . Just bums."

THE BOWERY 41

"Some days you can make four, maybe five bucks cleaning windshields . . . A sunny day after a good rain, got to be nice out too. If it's cold they keep the windows rolled up . . . Same if it's too hot. Everything's air conditioned today . . . The best used to be Frankie. He died right over there . . . A bunch of kids, hot-rodding, thought he'd get out of the way. . . He'd put up a real show . . . Dance a little, spoke good too, didn't scare people . . . . . . I remember one hot summer day, a really slick dude in one of them little sports cars with the top down come to a stop right over there at Delancy. . . . That car couldn't have been a day old, well that dude sees Frankie coming with this greasy rag . . . You should have seen it . . . First off he starts screaming and then he starts begging Frankie not to touch the car, but Frankie he's still coming . . . Finally this guy jumps out of the car, doesn't even open the door. He runs up to where Frankie is looking at his headlights and digs into his pockets and gives Frankie a five dollar bill if he'll promise not to touch the car. . . . Now that doesn't happen every day mind you, but you can make a good buck down here . . . If the weather's right."

"That's something! I come from Philadelphia too. 8th and Allen, out by the old federal pen . . . Lived there till 'fortyeight' when my wife left me. . . . Got two kids . . . They're living with their aunt and uncle . . . They're better there. I take care of 'em though. Yeah, I get an allotment and I send them every bit of it . . . I don't never touch it, none of it . . . You gotta believe that. I never touch none of it . . . I take care of them kids. . . . I got money uptown too . . . I'll tell you something, I give them most of that too, I only keep enough for food . . . That's all I need, just a little bit for food . . . Twentyone years in the navy, when the kids come of age the allotment stops . . . I don't know what I'm going to do then."

"Don't give me that. I know, I know bullshit . . . Where you going to sleep tonight???. . . You got a warm bed you're going to, right? . . . You ain't that bad looking you probably got a woman too . . . You wanna see where I'm going to sleep ???. . . Come on . . . I take this piece of cardboard and put it down in the hallway here, that way I don't have to sleep on the floor. You see, some of the guys come in here during the day and shit in the hallways of these abandoned buildings . . . It ain't that bad kid . . . Come here, look I'll show you . . . See right there . . . It ain't much of a shit. None of these guys eat enought to shit decent so a piece of cardboard's enough . . . Hey!!! I come and go as I please and it's a roof over my head. I'm a winner, right?"

"What are you drinking?"

"White port."

"Can I buy you one?"

"Thanks."

"What's your name?"

"Duke Miller."

"It's been good talking to you but I got to go back and find him."

"Who?"

"... Ah ... The guy I was with earlier ... ah ... Pete! I got to go find Pete ... we're buddies ... I got to find him because he ain't got nobody else ... He'd die out there by himself ... Lost his shoes this morning. How the Hell do you lose your shoes ... You seen him. He ain't got no shoes on ... A month or so it starts getting cold and he keeps up like this he ain't going to make the winter ... I better go find him."

"Yes Sir! I'll pose for you Sir! Never taken nothing from no one, No Sir! Never begged, never begged. Never taken nothing, No Sir! . . . . Yes Sir, you take my picture Sir. Yes Sir! Where do you want me Sir? Here Sir?. . . Never taken nothing, No Sir! Been a hard working man all my life Sir . . . Yes Sir, Never taken nothing No Sir!!! "

"You want me just ask anybody on the Bowery for the Polack."

"You a Polack?"

"I ain't a Polack . . . I'm THE Polack!!"

"You use a hot dog?"

"Yeah, I can use a hot dog."

"Can you make it down to the corner?"

"What do you think? I ain't a man?? I can walk from here to wherever you say . . . Drunk or sober!!"

"Easy. Easy there. You O.K.?"

"Yeah. I'm O.K. . . Where you want me to walk to?"

"The corner . . . For a dog?"

"Oh yeah. Let's go . . . I'll tell you something . . . Rather than a dog . . . I could use a pint of wine."

THE BOWERY 57

> Naw! You're shooting it all wrong. All you got in the picture is a drunk . . .
> You should get the entire place in. Show the happiness and gayiety; some of
> the pictures on the wall, the jukebox and pool table . . . then you show the
> drunk along with them.

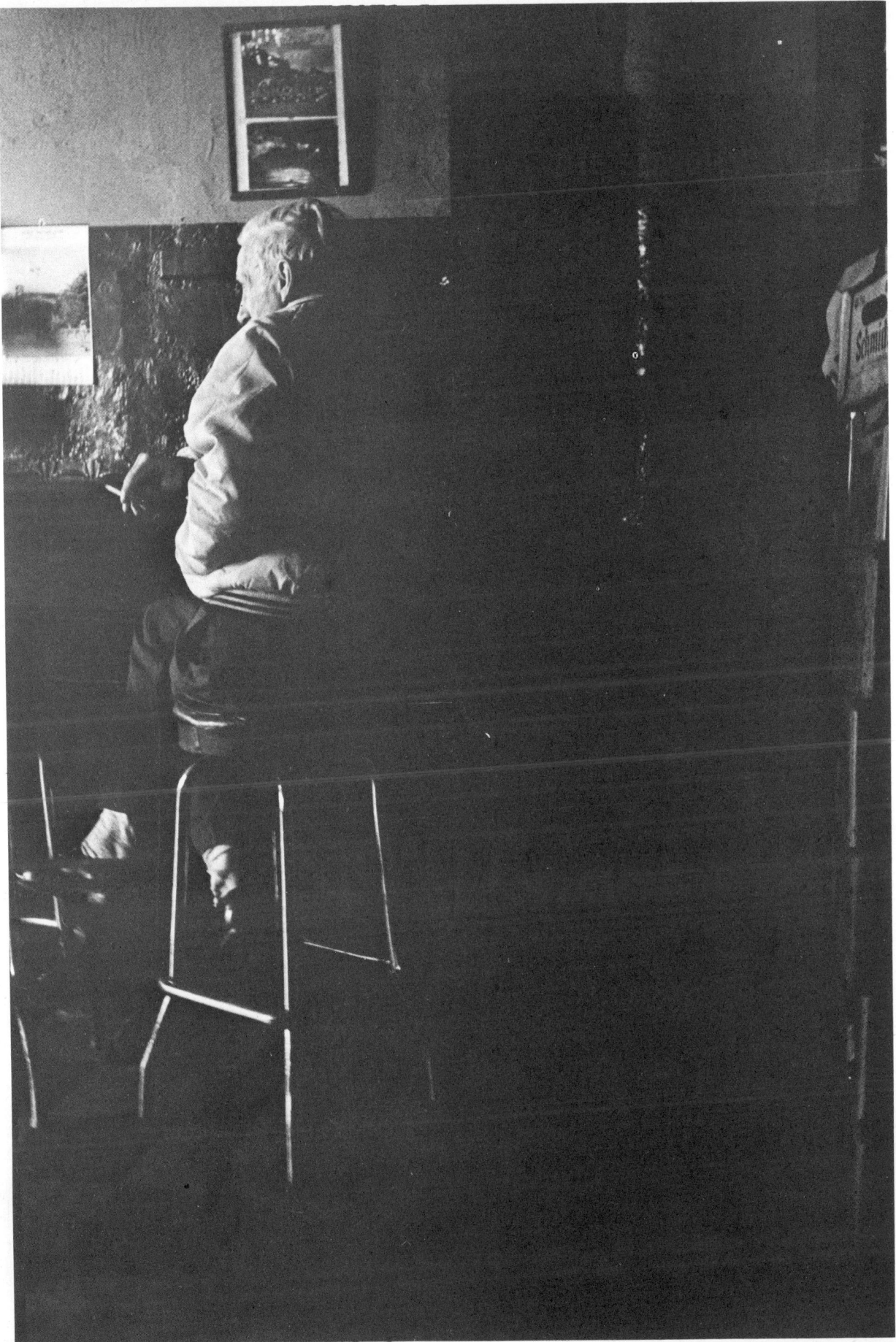

"Wait a minute, I think you got things wrong. I didn't say it was the greatest way in the world to make a living. I'd much rather be a head waiter in Miami Beach, but as it turns out that ain't what I do for a living. I buy things from bums and sell things to other bums, and like they say, . . . It's a living."

"After you take care of survival, next is sex. Last week I go down to Delancey and I give this whore fifteen dollars, spent like a sailor . . . Look at this!!!! Right here!!! She loses it all over my pants. I told her she was the worst fuckin sucker in the city of New York. . . . Ya know what she says to me??. . . <u>Don't spread it around.</u> Truth!!! So help me God!"

"The money ain't rough. All you got to do is look 'em in the eye . . . If they look back you got 'em . . . 'cause the only thing he's seeing in your eyes is himself . . . It ain't.generosity it's selfishness."

"Tough?? . . . Don't make me laugh. To everyone else he's Big Bad Bill but to me he ain't nothing but Sweet William."

No!! Now get the hell out of here . . . How many times I got to tell you Bimmies I don't buy shoes!"

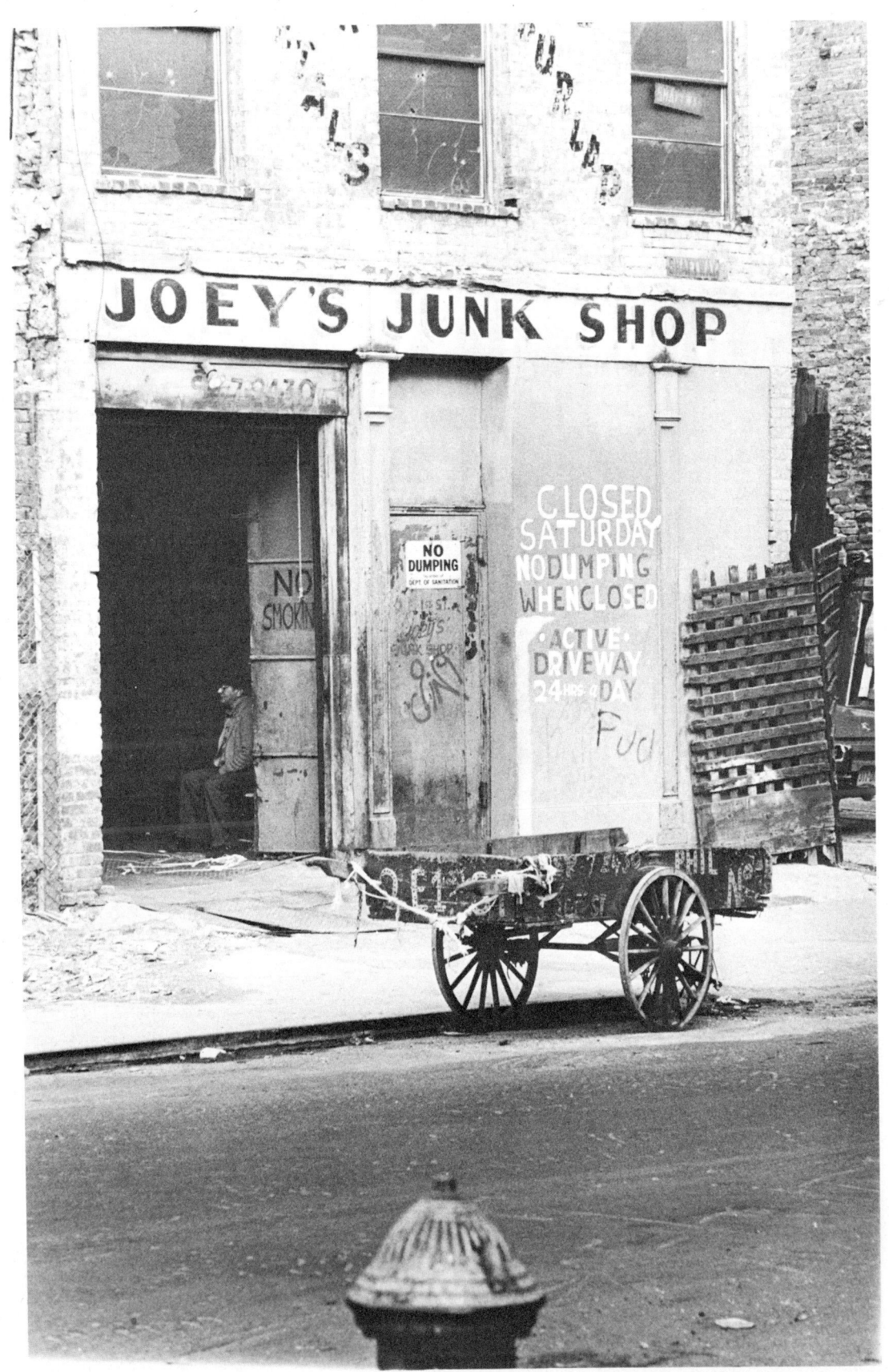

"I was in Baltimore in 1952 and I met the most beautiful girl in the world. She was as beautiful as the birth of spring . . . The most beautiful girl in the world . . . I married her and we had a child and then through my own carelessness she divorced me."

"Hey Pegleg, answer me for real, is Gigi beautiful?"

"You mean the guy who comes in here dressed up like a broad?"

"No Gigi!"

"That's who I'm talking about."

"That ain't Gigi."

"What is it with you? The guy's got this hang up on dresses but he's so ugly he's got to come down here with the bums. You're the only guy on the Bowery don't know it."

"That ain't the truth Pegleg."

"Christ sake he learned to put on makeup from a paving contractor . . . You blind or something???"

"She buys me drinks."

"Of course he does. You gotta be so fuckin blind you can't see you own hand or you'll know you're dating the washroom attendant at the Commodore!!"

"So when he comes into the tent I says to him general and he says corporal . . . he never knowed I was busted from top . . . What the fuck and they bring in the heavy stuff; New guns. Them Krauts is good but we kicked their ass from here to Berlin and back. What the fuck do you want General . . . I don't give a shit if you are a Colonel . . . Up to my ass in mud and Murphy wants to know where the rations is . . . Big new guns . . . What the fuck . . . The 101st. That's who!!!!! . . . Don't give me no shit about a General . . . We're all going home soon, you know that."

"A man who beats a woman is no man at all . . . I never touched no woman no Sir . . . never! . . .'course you don't find many women down here . . . 'cept for the hookers down on Canal. Some of them could use a beating . . . I never touched one though . . . Not me. Never touched a woman."

"Not your wife?"

"Not me . . . No matter how drunk she got, never touched her . . . I sure could use a drink."

"Come on, I'll buy you a beer."

"Naw. I can't go into the bars. They won't serve you on crutches. It's against the law, that's what they say . . . You got to go to a store . . . Hell, sometimes they won't even serve you in there . . . I really could use a drink."

"How'd you hurt the leg?"

"I got hit by a truck."

"Don't give him that shit!! You were asleep and he backed over you!"

"That ain't the truth Swede!! . . . You know that ain't the God Damned truth. Now tell the man . . . It don't make no difference anyway. I'm suing the son of a bitch . . . I'll get plenty too. Be out of here soon . . . Could you do me a big favor and go down to the store and see me through for a pint? . . . It'd help me out a lot, it sure would. There ain't much a man on crutches can do . . . I'll be out of here soon, though."

"You do start servin niggers, I'm drinking somewhere else."

"Hate to lose you, you're buck and a half a day."

"Sell wine at the right price to the next one and see how long I stay."

"I'll serve whoever I damn well please. . . . Besides, what's so wrong about it?"

"You're on that side of the bar . . . How'd you like to sit next to one of 'em?"

"I'm going to take you to meet Cathy . . . I love her . . . She don't know it of course. I think she likes me though."

"Does she live around here?"

"Naw. Girls like that don't live around here. She's a teller at the First National City Bank. I go every day just to look at her. Sometimes if I'm cleaned up enough I go in and talk to her . . . I had a friend who used to steal things from UPS for me to take to her . . . You know, toasters, that sort of thing. I gave her three toasters already . . . He's dead now though . . . Now, sometimes, I get enough money to buy flowers for her. She likes carnations best."

"Naw . . . Things ain't going too good. . . I seem to let my emotions carry me away . . . I can't seem to get ahold . . . I try too . . . . Thanks for asking. . . . I appreciate that."

THE BOWERY 83

"There's lots of things that's rough, but I'll tell you, when you're drunk stupid things is rough . . . Like standing up . . . there's more to it though, . . . It ain't just standing up, it's saving your life; 'Cause if you don't get up the car's going to run over you . . . or you're going to pass out an freeze . . . or . . . You're just going to die . . . Sometimes you just know if you don't stand up you're going to die."

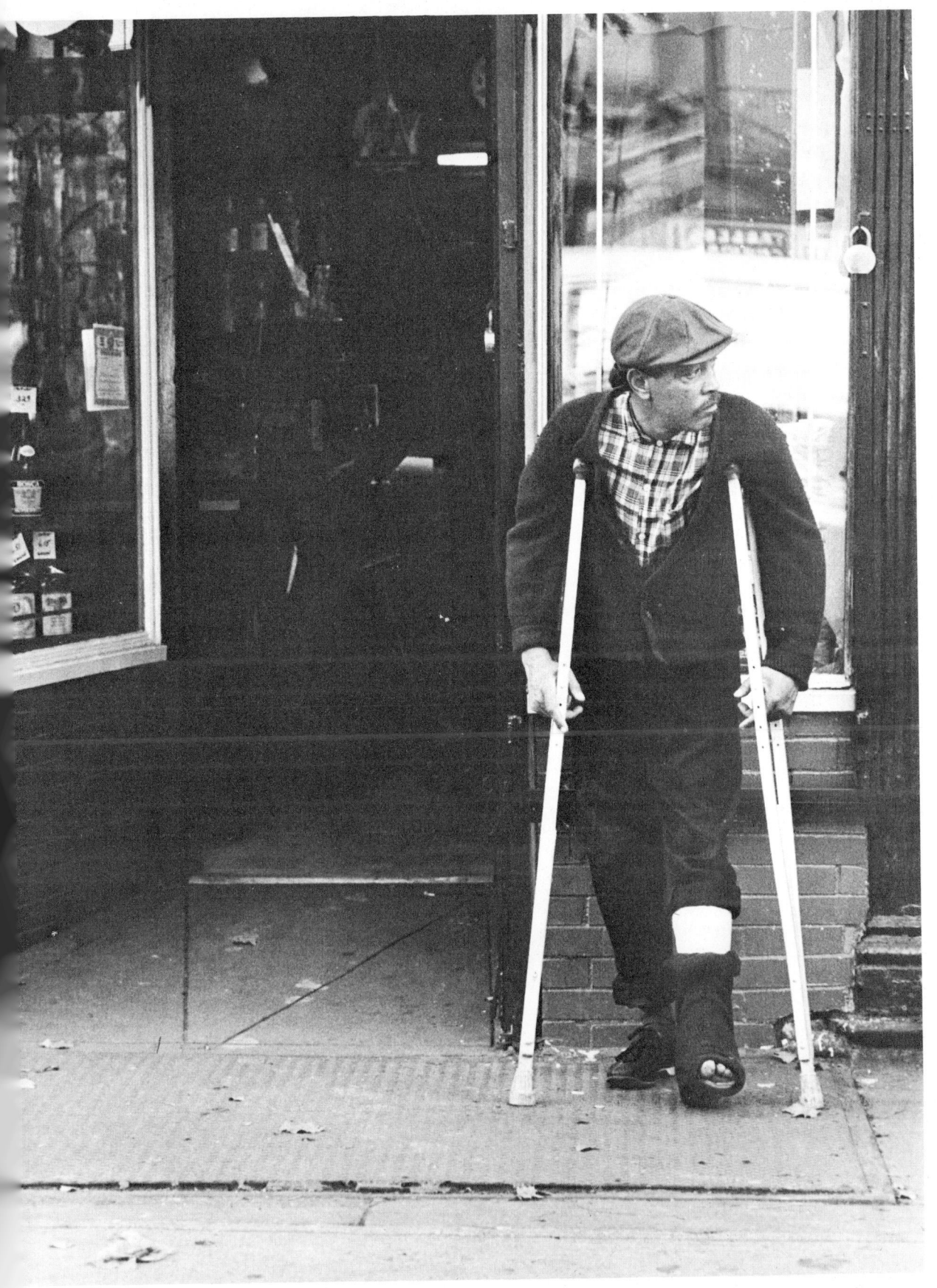

"Thanks pal I really appreciate this. Where you going? YOOOOOOUUUUUU want to come in and have a drink with me? . . . I'd sure like to HAAAAAAVE you come in and have one."

"No thanks."

"OK. SOOOOOOO Long."

"Every bar's got a cat, he's Mickey . . . Just had the best looking litter a kittens . . . Black and white just like him . . . I guess we should call her something else but . . . It'd be sort a unfair to all the guys in here . . . As far as they're concerned, that's Mickey . . . They really love him too . . . Hell, he's all they got . . . You ought to see 'em back there cooing over those kittens, you'd think they was the father."

"I can't work. The mind's gone . . . Shot down . . . I was sober, cold with 1800 bucks and I lost it . . . It's no good no more . . . I can't do it."

"Tough getting the wine sometimes?"

"What the hell are you talking about? If it's so tough to get drunk how in the name of hell do you think so many no talent bums got drunk . . . Getting drunk's easy, it's staying sober that's rough."

"You tried it?"

"Sure I tried it . . . You want to know what it's like? Go on around the corner . . . Come on I'll show you . . . There! Look at 'em!! They bring 'em in here and dry 'em out and let 'em sort clothes and furniture. Look at 'em!! Sittin there starin at each other, too afraid to say nothing . . . It's good they keep 'em close, every time I think I might dry out I come over here and talk myself out of it . . . Look at 'em!!!!!"

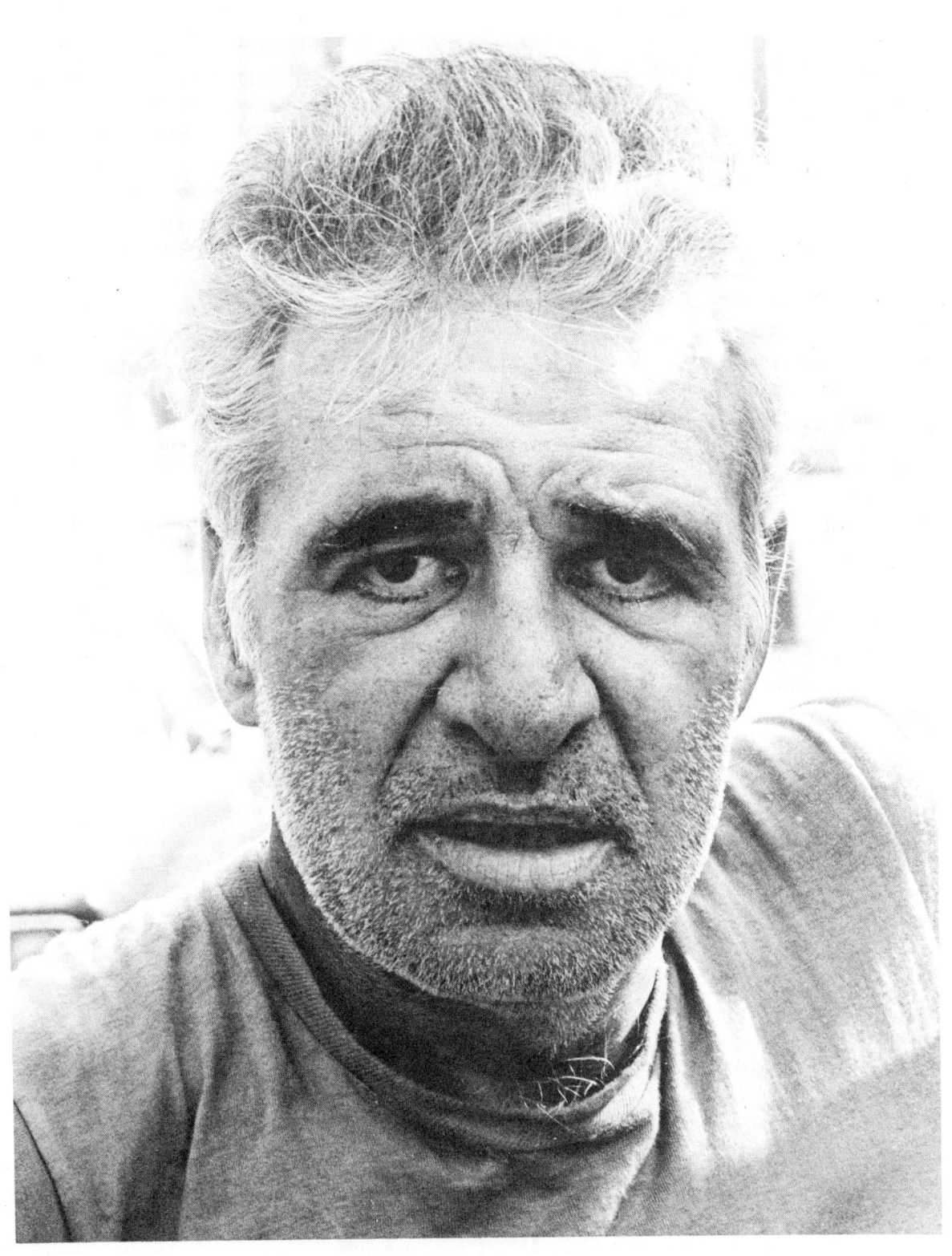

THE BOWERY

"Wow!... Will you look at that. That looks tight... A tight little box, that's what I need."

"Why do you talk like that? What's wrong with you?... It ain't no way to be talking about a woman."

"She's a whore!"

"I don't like to hear it."

"You might not like to hear it, but you'd like to get it."

"You got no respect for nothing?? I don't want to hear that kind of talk."

"I'd like to get it that's for sure."

"What would you do with it if you did?"

"I'd eat it."

"That's a terrible way to talk about a woman."

"They're all whores. I heard you say that yourself."

"Terrible way to talk."

THE BOWERY

"I'd let you take my picture, but you see a lot of us got influential families and they don't like to have our picture's taken . . . You know what I mean? . . . 'cause if they recognize us you're in big trouble and I don't want to see you get in big trouble."

"Hey! . . . You can take my picture if you promise it'll never get to Ireland."

"I promise."

" 'cause if my mother seen it it'd break her heart."

"I promise."

"I ain't seen her in thirty seven years but she'd know me."

"Is she still alive?"

"Yeah. She's still alive . . . I ain't heard nothing from her in twenty years . . . I mean to write her . . . I mean to write her all the time . . . Yeah, I'm sure she's still alive . . . I don't know what I'd do if she wasn't."

"You put a drunk behind the bar and it's like putting the fox in the chicken coop!! " . . . Well, that ain't the way it is . . . Oh, he gets drunk the first day maybe, but after that he's good . . . A married man, he's stealing for his wife and kids. But who's a drunk going to steal for . . . The only thing he wants is booze and he's up to his ass in it . . . 'Course all these guys are shot down an every so often they go off the deep end for a week or so and you got to nurse them back . . . But a drunk'll never steal from you . . . I know. I keep a good eye on 'em and I never seen one steal yet.

"Where's the last kitten ?!?!"

"Somebody stole it."

"You sure?"

"You don't see it, it's gone."

"I find the son of a bitch did that I'll break him in half . . . What kind of a miserable son of a bitch would do a thing like that . . . It's OK Mickey, I'm going out and find the miserable son of a bitch who done it and bring that kitten back . . . What kind of a miserable . . . "

"Will you shut up . . . I seen you damn near kill a man for a quarter and now you're sittin' here slobbering over some damn cat!"

"It weren't a cat!! . . . It was a kitten."

Listen to him!!! . . . . Tough. We got to listen to how mean he is again? . . . . Will you listen to that? The male animal in full cry, his mother comes through that door right now he'll weep like a baby.

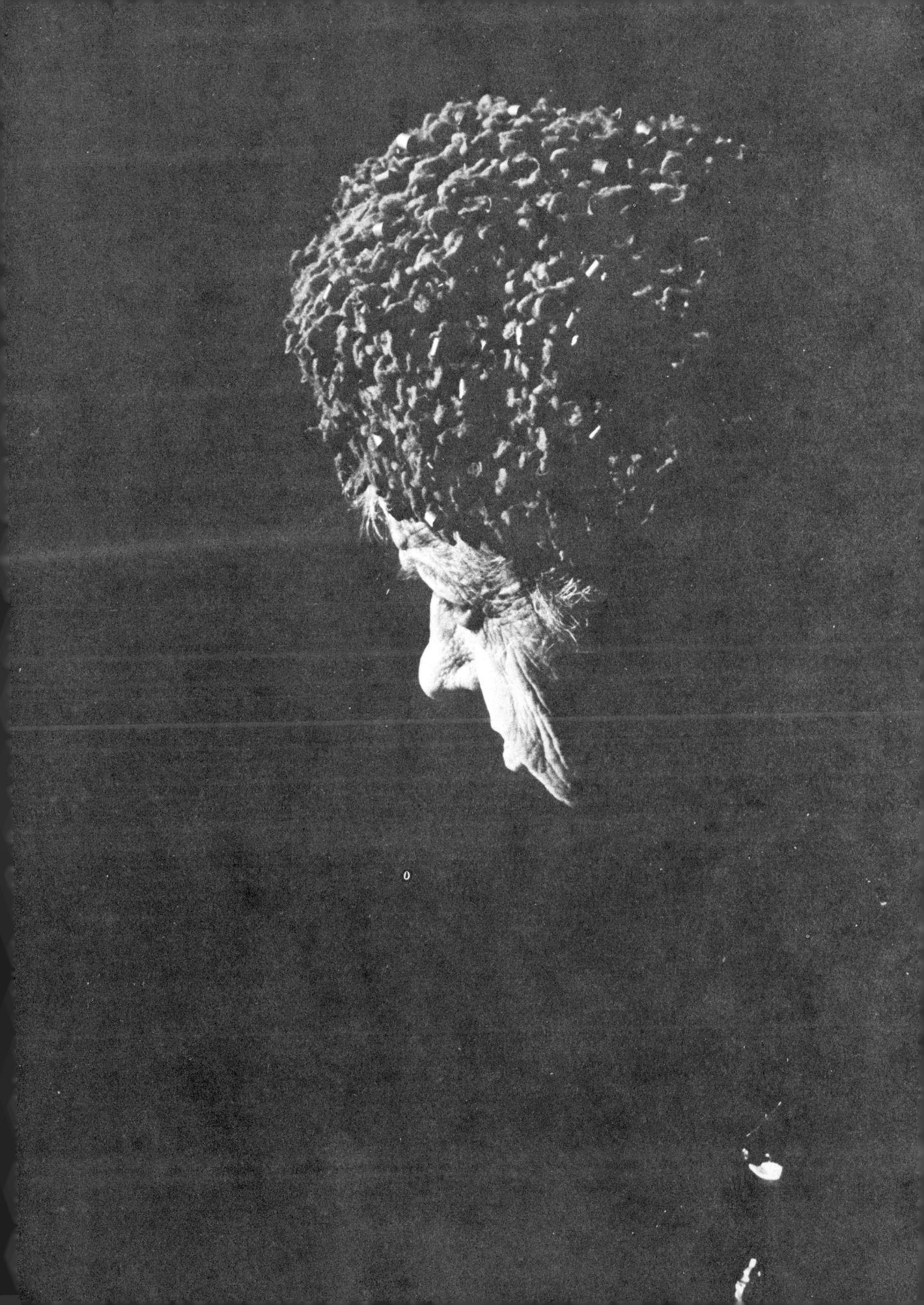

"As a bartender he's OK but I'll tell ya . . . As a person he's what you get out of an empty glass."

THE BOWERY 111

THANKSGIVING DAY 1974

What have I got to be thankful for?... I'm still alive, that's one thing......
but I didn't even get a good meal down at the mission.

THE BOWERY 113

"You think you're so fucking smart? 1963!!!! Name the supreme court justices!"

"... Earl Warren ..."

"In alphabetical order!!!! ... You don't know do you?!! ... All right ... First you got Hugo Black. He was an Alabama segregationalist. Next you got Brennan, then you got a good man; Tom Clark, always fair, you can't take that away from him ... All right, who comes next???? .. The biggest cocksmith in the city of Washington ... Come on !!!!"

"Douglas?"

"At least you know something ... Next comes a small person but a big man in his own right ... Harlaan ... Then Goldberg ... They got rid of him because they don't like Jews ... Now here's a toughie, not many people know him because he's kinda quiet; Stewart ... Then there's the guy who fooled them all ... The Governor of California ..."

"Warren."

"Two out of nine is pretty piss poor ... Now!! What was the landmark decision of 1963???"

"I don't know."

"You ever hear of Clarence Gideon??"

"You mean the bibles?"

"Not the bibles you fucking idiot. He was an indigent carpenter in Georgia ..."

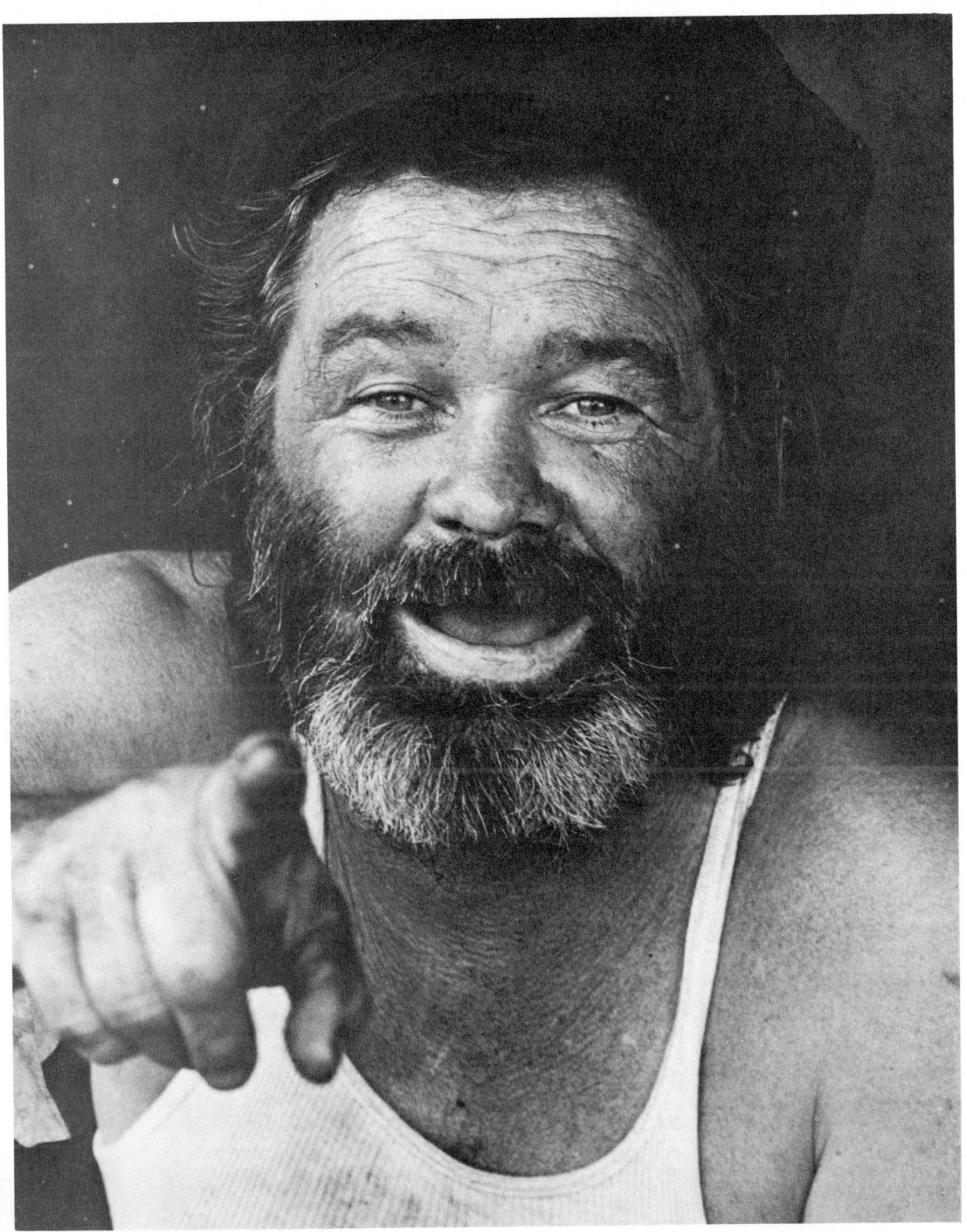

Naw! . . . . Leave him . . . . . . It ain't going to freeze tonight anyway . . .
. . . . is it?

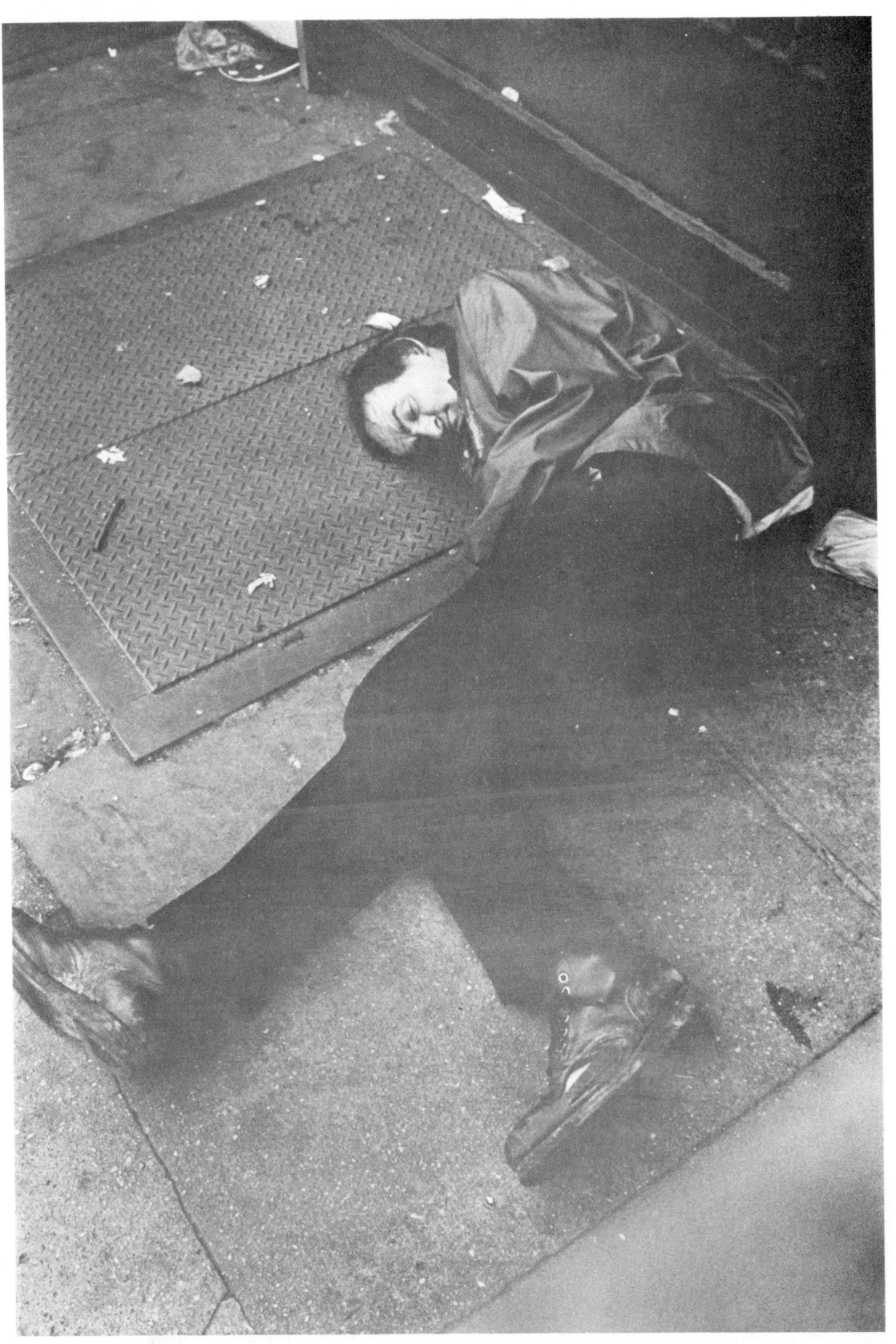

Hope I can get enough to get a room tonight . . . The nurse down at the welfare says it's gettin too cold to sleep out anymore . . . I got this thing with my lung . . . No one seems to know what to do . . . wish they could stop the coughing though. Yesterday I coughed so bad I thought I was going to . . . . . . I just wish they could do something about it.

"I was coming back to the City last month and I stopped in this little road side bar in Long Branch, don't know the name of it, . . . had red curtains I think, . . . anyway there was this girl singing there with a little combo. A lot of that guitar stuff, loud, you know. I don't like it much but this place seemed to be doing a good business . . . After she'd sung a couple of numbers I went up to her and told her she was the best singer I ever heard since Peggy Lee. Yup, that's right, Peggy Lee . . . And I know too, I used to book all the acts into the Watergap Hotel in Atlantic City . . . Let me see, that was in the thirties . . . I owned a part of the place then . . . Nice place, big porches you could sit on, real nice . . . I long since drunk up my share of the place, but I'm telling you I know talent and this girl was as good as Peggy Lee . . . We had a good time in that bar, . . . wish I could remember the name . . . Stayed there till two in the morning listening to that girl, . . . Lost all my money there. Had to sell most of my clothes to get back into the city but, I'll tell you that girl could sing."

THE BOWERY 121

Hey mister could you spare . . . . . . Mister? . . . . . Hey Mister! . . . . Hey! . . . . HEY!!!

I don't want the money . . . I want you to come and have a drink with me. . . . . .I'm lonely.

128 THE BOWERY

I don't care where you put 'im . . . Just get him out of the doorway.
Hell, roll him out in the street!

See that?... Now that's stupid... Young kid, still thinks he can fall out anywhere... Watch it. Someone's goin to steal his clothes the minute it's dark... Hell they might even kill him.... No reason why they shouldn't.

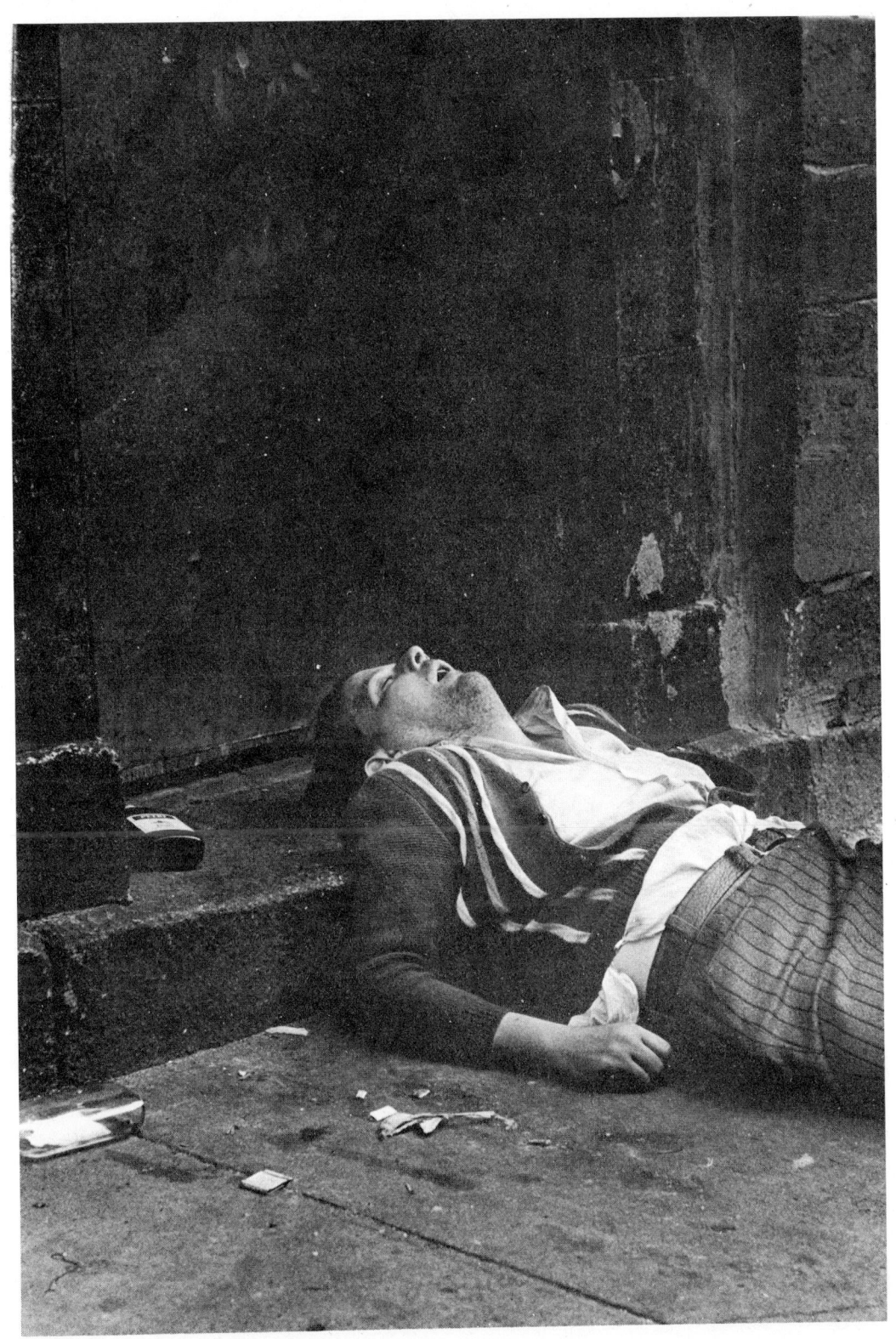

I don't know what to do . . . I'd get out but I know I'm just comin' back again. . . . Got to be a way to get out for good.

"Door, door . . . got to find a door . . . Sun set, snow, sleet . . . tearing my face . . . my face . . . Light, no light, sun gone . . . got to find a door. . . got to find a knob that turns . . . got to . . . got to . . . Don't want to freeze . . . not today, no . . . don't want to die . . . not today . . . Booze wearing off . . . Head hurts. Sleet, sleet . . . Hands, cold . . . numb . . . numb . . . warm, warm . . . Hands won't close . . Can't turn knob . . . can't turn . . . Door is open. . . . OPEN!! . . . CAN'T TURN KNOB!!!! . . . this is open . . . can't grip . . . hands won't close . . . sleet . . . SLEET!!! . . . OPEN!! . . . God Damn it can't turn knob . . . . PLEASE!!!!! . . . . . . I DON'T WANT TO FREEZE!!! . . . PLEASE!!! . . . . don't want to freeze . . . don't want to cry . . . can't go on . . . don't want to die today.

"Is he all right Officer?"

"He's better off than the rest of 'em . . . Sure is yellow, ain't he?"

"Yeah . . . Is he dead?"

"Stiff."

"Where does he go from here?"

"Why? You want him? . . . The wagon'll be along in a moment they take 'em up to the morgue at Bellvue . . . The kids who're going to be doctors get to cut 'em up . . . There probably ain't much left to look at inside of him though."

2050-50M-403060(74) 346

CITY OF NEW YORK
OFFICE OF CHIEF MEDICAL EXAMINER

Case No. 002093

Time Received: **RECEIVED** '74 DEC 18 AM 8:16 CHIEF MEDICAL EXAMINER

BOROUGH OF ....

NOTICE OF DEATH

Police _Michael O'Riley_ (Name of Officer)   Precinct No. _8_

Hospital .... (Name)   (Doctor reporting case)

Private Physician .... (Name) (Address) (Tel. No.)

Reported by: Other .... (Name) (Address) (Friend, Relative, Funeral Director, Health Dept.)

NAME OF DECEASED _Unknown White Male_   AGE _55_   SEX _M_

USUAL RESIDENCE ....   Occupation ....   Race _W_

PLACE OF DEATH _250 Bowery_   APT.#   TEL.#

If moved from public place to mortuary by police, give precinct number _8_

Date and time of Admission in Hospital Cases .... Att. Physician ....

Previous private medical attention, if any, by Dr. .... Address .... Tel.# ....

DATE and TIME of DEATH	NOTIFIED	TIME	DISPOSITION
12:50 PM 11/28/74	Med. Examiner Med. Investigator		☐ Certified at scene ☒ Ordered to M. E. Mortuary ☐ No Case ☐ Cremation
	(Name)		(Check)

Circumstances and pertinent information leading to reporting of case ....
(In hospital cremation cases include whether body was autopsied)

Lying face-up on sidewalk at 250 Bowery — cuts on face + hands — fully clothed ... No shoes

J.P. Nelson
Clerk

142   **THE BOWERY**

ME-2052-10M-702100(73) 346

THE CITY OF NEW YORK
OFFICE OF CHIEF MEDICAL EXAMINER

MORTUARY COMPARTMENT CARD

COMPARTMENT NUMBER 30

Name Unknown White Male

Age 50 Color White Date of Death 11/28/74

Received from City Heart Date Received 11/28/74

Place of Death 250 Bowery

"Not that many of them die in the streets. Most die in one of the city hospitals, then they're sent here . . . We keep them until we find out who they are or if no one claims them they go to the University Medical schools. They're passed out on an allotment basis. If they don't go there they're buried in Potter's Field. It's out on Hart's Island. You take a ferry across from either Bronx or Queens . . . You know who could tell you? Call the Department of Corrections out on Riker's Island. They got the inmates out there and they bury them."

148   THE BOWERY

TECHNICAL INFORMATION:

Camera: Nikon F

Lenses: 21 m.m. Nikkor
35 m.m. Nikkor
105 m.m. Nikkor
200 m.m. Nikkor
50 m.m. Nikkor

Paper and Chemicals: Kodak